Earthling Study Skills

Sarah Fleming

Zock

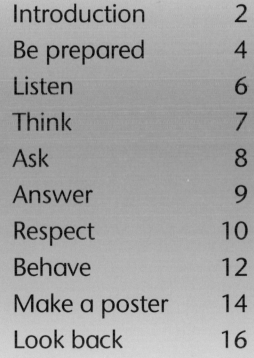

Fob

Voll

Zem

Spim

Contents

Kizz

Trax

Muss

Chod

In A Classroom Far Away on Planet Zog...

We will go on our school trip to Earth in ten days' time...

SCHOOL ON EARTH

FOOD ON EARTH

Earthling clothes

Whoopee!

A WEEK ON EARTH
SCHOOL TRIPS FOR YEAR 040

In here, there is a classroom like an Earth classroom for you to work in today. You will get a chance to work in a real Earth classroom when we go to Earth.

DIFFERENCES BETWEEN PLANET ZOG AND PLANET EARTH

WHAT ON EARTH?

TRAVEL ON EARTH

Hooray!

Always keep a pencil near you.

Listen to your teacher.

Think about what you're doing.

Ask questions.

Answer questions.

Zem! Chod!

I know! I Know!

Don't ask me!

Look, like this! Yes, Kizz?

Try to answer questions if you can.

I think the answer is that...

If I want to answer a question, I'll put up my hand.

9

Respect yourself.

Behave in the dining room.

In here we've made an Earth school dining room.

Make a poster.

Things You Should Do

Make a poster about earth school rules. These are the things you should do.

- ★ Find a big piece of paper.
- ★ Use bright colours.
- ★ Think of a heading.
- ★ Think of pictures.
- ★ Write large.
- ★ Write clearly.
- ★ Use simple sentences.
- ★ Write what to do, *not* what not to do.

Use some of these words on your poster:

answer

ask

behave

listen

respect

think

tidy

These words are all in this book. You can use the rules from the book in your poster. Can you think of some more of your own?

☆——— SCHOOL RULES RAP ———✿

Let's make the cleanest coolest school
so everyone is happy
Please put your books away and keep the library tidy
If there's someone hurt, then help them out
Walk up the stairs, and you'll always be safe
Sweep up that mess, and put it in its place